Robert Kelley Weeks

Episodes and Lyric Pieces

Robert Kelley Weeks

Episodes and Lyric Pieces

ISBN/EAN: 9783744652834

Printed in Europe, USA, Canada, Australia, Japan

Cover: Foto ©Thomas Meinert / pixelio.de

More available books at **www.hansebooks.com**

EPISODES

AND

LYRIC PIECES.

BY

ROBERT KELLEY WEEKS.

NEW YORK:
LEYPOLDT & HOLT.
1870.

Entered according to Act of Congress, in the year 1870, by
ROBERT KELLEY WEEKS,
In the Office of the Librarian of Congress at Washington.

THE NEW YORK PRINTING COMPANY,
81, 83, *and* 85 *Centre Street,*
NEW YORK.

CONTENTS.

PART FIRST.

	PAGE
The Return of Paris,	3
Song,	10
King Ægeus,	11
In Corinth,	13
In Collatia,	22
Medusa,	28
A Winter Evening,	30
A Spring Morning,	35
Shadows,	36
A Change,	37
Ad Finem,	39
The New Narcissus,	41
A Question,	42
Pilgrimage,	45
Sir Gawaine's Love,	57
Her Name,	75

	PAGE
In Winter,	76
Greenhouse Flowers,	77
Till Spring,	79
In Nubibus,	84
A Pause,	87
Too Late,	89
Autumn Song,	90
Undersong,	91
A Prodigal,	93
Maggior Dolore,	96
Gone,	99
The Moral,	101
The End,	102

PART SECOND.

Vita Vitalis,	105
A Day,	110
The River,	115
"In the Springtime,"	117
In Early April,	118
In May,	119
Spring Song,	121
May Song,	123

CONTENTS.

	PAGE
Moonlight in May,	125
In the Meadow,	126
By the Lake,	127
By the Bay,	128
The Mist,	129
Rara Avis,	132
The Katydid,	133
A Vine,	135
On the Beach,	136
A Glimpse of Life,	137
My Star,	138
Man and Nature,	139
Calm and Cold,	141
Winter Sunrise,	142
Winter Sunset,	143
By the Fireside,	144
The Men of Crete,	145
The Lion of Lucerne,	146
My Place,	148
Ad Amicum,	164

The "Return of Paris" was suggested by Mr. Cox's tale of Œnone in the "Tales of the Gods and Heroes." The particular version of a story, which Lecky says is of frequent occurrence in accounts of the early Christians, which I have used in the "In Corinth," is one that I found accidentally in Hippolytus (vol. 2, p. 96—vol. IX. of the Ante-Nicene Library), *who represents the girl as "a certain most noble and beautiful maiden in the city of Corinth," whom the "young man Magistrianus," a Christian also, saves in the way indicated in the poem. I have preferred to think of the young man as a Pagan (with a touch of modern sentiment), who does for love what Hippolytus says the Christian did, striving "nobly for his own immortal soul." Sir Gawaine is, of course, an anachronistic consideration (I hope not too curious a one) of the old ballad in Percy. In writing the "Maggior Dolore" (perhaps I may as well say) I was probably thinking quite as much of the Third Canto of the Inferno as of the Fifth.*

PART FIRST.

WITH MEN AND WOMEN.

POEMS

THE RETURN OF PARIS.

I STUMBLED thrice, and twice I fell and lay
Moaning and faint, and yet I did not pray
To any God or Goddess of them all;
Because I never doubted, climb or crawl,
That I should reach the fountain and the tall
One old familiar pine-tree, where I lay
Prone on my face, with outstretched hands, you say,
Fallen once again—this time against the goal.
And now, what shall I pray for? since my whole
Wish is accomplished, and I have your face
Once more by mine in the remembered place,
And the cool hand laid on my head aright,
A little while before I die to-night.

For surely I am dying: not a vein
But has received the poison and the pain
Of Philoctetes' arrow.—Oh! I heard
The hissing of the vengeance long deferred,
And felt it smite me, and not smite me dead;
And all at once the very words you said
Too long ago returned to me once more—
When, as you shall be, you are wounded sore,
Come back to me, and I will cure you then,
Whom none but I can cure: and once again,
Sweet! I am with you, and am cured by you,
And by you only; and yet it is true
That I must die, Œnone. So it is,
And better that it is so! Hark to this.
How good it were, if we could live once more
The old sweet life we found so sweet before—
Here in the mountain where we were so glad,
Ere I was cruel and ere you were sad!
How good it were could we begin again
The old sweet life just where we left it then!

A song, love;—but my singing voice is gone—
The one song that I made, the only one
After I left you to be mad so long;
(A marvellous thing to have made no other song!)
The only one—which, many months ago,
Came to me strangely with a soft and slow
Movement of music, which at first was sad,
But sad and sweet, and after only sad,
And then most bitter, as its death gave birth
To a low laughter of uneasy mirth—
Made of blent noises that the night-winds bore,
The lapse of waves upon the dusky shore,
The creaking of the tackle, and the stir
Of threatening banners where the camp-fires were
About the armies, that no such a charm
As a regretful love-song could disarm,
And bring to life the heroes that were slain,
And make the war as if it were a vain
Noise in the night that at the morn is not,
And all the Past a dream that it begot.

The wind was right to laugh my song away!

And then I thought—if only for a day
I might be with her, only for so long
As to be pardoned or (forgive the wrong)
Cursed by her there, and so get leave to die!
And here we are, Œnone, you and I!
Yes, we are here! why ever otherwhere?

Ah! why indeed? And yet, love, let me dare
Uncover my whole heart to you once more;
I think I never was so blest before—
Never so happy as I am to-day.
Not even, indeed, when in the early May
We found each other, and were quite too glad
To know the value of the love we had.
But now I seem to know it in my need,
Inhaling the full sweetness of it—freed
Now, for the first time, from its perfect flower;
Ah! quite too sweet to overlast its hour!

What more now shall I pray for? To be let
Live and not die? Ah! if we could forget
All but the Present and outlaw the Past!
And yet I know not—could the Present last
If quite cut off from all that gave it birth,
And not be changed, if changed to alien earth,
Into a Future that we know not of?
We will not ask : we have attained to Love—
Whatever grown from—which not all the years
Past or to come, nor memories nor fears,
Can rob us of forever, nor make less.
No praying then—but only thankfulness!

No sound floats hither from the smoky plain:
Turn me a little—never mind the pain—
I see it now. And that was Ilion then!
The accursed city in the mouths of men,
Whose mouths are swift to interweave its name
With mine forever for a word of shame.
I never loved it, and it loved me not—

The fatal firebrand that itself begot
And tried to quench and could not—there it smokes!
And there the shed blood of its people soaks
Into the soil that they loved more than life.

Let the Gods answer, who decreed the strife!
But you, great-hearted, whom indeed I loved—
Brother and friend, by whom, if unapproved,
I was loved sometime in the upper air—
Will you turn from me when I meet you there
And greet you, Hector, in the other world?
Will you turn from me, with lip coldly curled,
And frank eyes hardened?—

                    I accept the sign!
Lo you! Œnone, where the gloomy line
Of the slow clouds is broken, and a bright
Gleam, like a smile, steals softly into sight
And grows to a glory in the increasing sky!

Nay, you are right, love! What have you and I
To do with Past or Future, who have for boon
So rich a Present, to exhaust so soon
Between the daylight and the afterglow?
The last cloud passes, and how calm I grow!
And now—if I should close my eyes, my love,
And seem to sleep a little, and not move
Until the sky has got its perfect gold,
You will not think me dying while I hold
Your hand thus closely? Kiss me now. Again!
Past chance of change—just where we left it
    then.

ŒNONE.

I had him last! I had him first and last!
His morning beauty and his evening charm!
Oh, Love! triumphant over all the Past,
What Death can daunt you, or what Future
    harm?

SONG.

An under-cloud that half reveals,
    Half hides a splendid star;
(Even then more clear than others are,
    As always queenlier.)
Such was my love to her.

A wilting wind that bends a rose
    Not very long nor far;
(Even then more fresh than others are,
    As always lovelier.)
Such was my love to her.

O star of stars, as clear and high!
    O rose of roses, none the less!
The cloud is blown out of the sky,
    The wind is in the wilderness.

KING ÆGEUS.

(A Fragment.)

IT was a day of light; the gracious sun
  Filled full of light the insatiate Autumn air,
And streamed in splendour on the exulting sea,
Till the low waves, blent by the rippling breeze,
Near by showed blinding silver—but beyond,
The laughter of innumerable eyes
That winked in an embarrassment of joy.
Above, the undazzled sky was calm, was blue,
With here and there a lonely dimpled cloud,
White as the flying sea-foam whence it sprang—
Slow wandering noiseless on its dreamy way,
Half heedless of the embracing wind's desire;

And on the land the sun smiled joyously,
The green fields took a brighter green, the grain
Rose panting broadly to the genial light,
And bending low, returned the golden smile;
All things were overfull of happy life,
And all the mingled noises in the air
Seemed vainly murmuring of the joy of earth:
Alone amid them all, the sad old king
Sat listening, and heard nothing but a sound
Of quivering silence in his empty ears—
Sat looking, and saw nothing but a want
Of anything to see in all the world,
Unfilled as yet by any little sail.

IN CORINTH.

LET me review it all before I sleep;
I am still too happy to be quiet yet,
And grudge to give one morsel of my joy,
Unrelished fully, to distorting dreams,
Or mere oblivion: let me taste it all
Slowly and thankfully from end to end,
And then the last before the final sleep
From which I wake to wait for her in heaven;
It must be so, I feel that it is so.

Before I ever held her by the hand,
Before I ever called her by her name,
Before I ever looked her in the face
I knew and loved her, as I knew and loved

All things whose loveliness makes men despair—
Despair and love, and never quite despair.
And when I met her first, a year ago,
And heard her voice and saw her mouth and eyes,
This is the love that I foresaw, I said,
And thrilled with joy to see her here at last;
Here and not here—for, when I looked again,
I saw the place she stood on, far aloof
From all of me except my merest dreams,
And scorned my littleness, and turned away
And let despair instruct me how to love.

But no despair could teach me to forget,
Nor utterly compel me to its will,
While yet my heart was tender to the touch
Of influences from the day and night,
The sunlight and the starlight, grass and trees,
And clouds and skies and waters, for the charm
With which all these allured me and repelled,

And saddened me, and quickened and consoled,
Still led me in a circle back to her
To whom all other loveliness referred.

I saw her very seldom in my life—
Too very seldom, as I used to say;
It irked me bitterly to waste the days
So far from Corinth and the sight of her.
And does it irk me now to think of this?
And shall I, as I used, accuse the Past,
And count it lost because not spent with her?
If I had seen her oftener, perhaps
It might have been far otherwise; but now,
How is it now? Is it not perfect now?
I would not have it otherwise.

                           And yet,
Glad as I am, yes, quite content and glad—
Perhaps, indeed, because I am so glad—

I cannot yet, quite yet, forget to dream
Of all that might have been. I wish I knew
More of that Heaven she spoke of. But
    enough—
It is enough; I will not lose in dreams
The recollection of what was and is.
It is enough for me to live to-night;
To-day is mine and yesterday is mine,
To-morrow shall ask questions of itself.

Day before yesterday I said, 'Tis now
A month since I have seen or heard of her;
To-morrow is the birth-day of my love:
A year ago to-morrow I first saw
And loved the only woman in the world.
She surely cannot love me; but the days
Fall from my life like withered leaves, and soon
What freshness will be left of all my youth?
I will go tell her all, and ask her leave
At least to be permitted to outwear

My life in some impossible attempt
To overcome the gulf and climb the height
That separates me from her; or at least,
I will go see her and not say a word,
See her once more and go away content,
And never vex her after. That is best—
See her once more and afterward no more.
And so it was; I saw her just once more,
And proved my love instead of speaking it.

She is quite safe, I know, and out of reach—
Quite out of reach of that accursed—God!
That I could kill him! She is surely safe.
But it is dreadful to remember now
How slight an error might have thwarted all.
But I was certain that I should succeed—
I never doubted once.

      When I first heard
That she was brought before that beastly Judge

For blasphemy against his foolish gods,
I knew what I was born for. When they said,
"'Tis a pretext, this charge of blasphemy,
'Tis not the first time he has played this game"
(I hate myself that it is not the last),
"He only wants to force her to his will"—
Not even then I doubted, tho' the words
Made my knees shake. I did not doubt at all,
But waited.

In the afternoon I learned
(Whether made blind by rage or keen by craft,
What matters it? I thwarted him at both),
That since she neither would deny her God
Nor take such pardon as he offered her,
That he had done a thing impossible—
Had sent her to a brothel with command
That any man who might be base enough—
I hardly can believe it even now!

I bargained for and bought her with a price.
That was a strange and bitter thing to do:
For every coin I could have better borne
To give a piece of my indignant heart.
It needed all the love I had for her
To save me from the frenzy of remorse,
And shame and pain which would have ruined all.
This too becomes a thing incredible—
A tale, a dream—I will not think of it.

But all the rest of it is sweet and good.
All was arranged, the friends and horses sure,
The dusk excluded and the stars aloft,
When I gave over watching and went in
And found her—on the birth-day of my love,
I thought of that—and as she raised her eyes,
Not shamefully but grandly, all the place
Seemed changed and sacred—a good place to be;

Not, as I called it while I watched outside,
A dung-hill darkened by a spotless rose,
Black mire made blacker by a speckless pearl,
Night's gloom made gloomier by a single star,
But night was morn, white marble was the mire,
And the dung-hill a garden having her.

She knew me in a moment, took my hand
And said, I thought--I knew that you would
 come.
What must we do?" I told her all the plan.
"You must disguise yourself with mask and cloak
To look like me; and when the street is clear,
Go boldly forth, and turning to the right,
Meet and be safe with one who says my name."
"And you?"—"I wait a while and watch my chance
To join you afterward." She smiled a strange,
Unnamable, sweet, melancholy smile,
And seemed to muse a moment, and then said,

"Yes, you are right!" and then, "You too believe,
As I do, that we meet our friends in Heaven,
And know each other after death, my friend?
Stoop down a little. I kiss you now and here,
And make you an appointment."

                                         So she said.

But here they say, that I must fight the beasts
To-morrow. To-morrow! I beat them yesterday.

IN COLLATIA.

THAT he were come, O God that he were come!
To wait and wait for him, and think and think,
And grow old thinking, while the lazy sun
Crawls inch by inch along the helpless sky—
I shall be gray and wrinkled before noon!
Ah! 'twas not thus I used to wait for him.
'Twas not thus yesterday, yet yesterday
Was not so beautiful a day as this.
Impossible that I can be so changed!
To dream a dream of evil, and awake
And half remember and wholly loathe and hate
And spurn the unasked, unwelcomed, alien thing,
How can that make one impure who was pure?
Was pure? is pure; is even purer now

By so much as the evil thing is loathed
More, more and more for that chance glimps
   of it.
Is good so slight a thing that at a touch
Evil can make it evil against its will?
Is to be pure no more than to escape
The passing touch of loathed impurity,
Mere bodily good-fortune?
                         Not in me!
I am Lucretia still!
                         No, I am not,
No more than this gnawed vine-leaf is the same
That it was yesterday before the worm
Crawled over and defiled it and destroyed.
Changed, changed and changed! and he too
   will be changed:
I am but a beginning, but a link
In a long chain of evil, but a means
To transmit pain and sorrow, and from me—
From me? O what am I become? From me!

Why do I turn me from the stainless sky
To dwell upon this miserable leaf,
Which while I hold I shudder at—and hold?
I lose myself, I stumble in the paths
Where I was once familiar, while a sense
Of intimacy with things hitherto
Unknown or known but to be shunned and
 spurned
Takes me with fascination, till I seem
To be but one of many whom I loathe,
But haply shall not always loathe as now!
There is some awful mystery in this,
Some dread relationship of good to bad,
Which whirls me from myself to think of it.

But I am not one of them, I am not,
I am not one of them. I am myself,
Lucretia still! insulted but not stained,
Insulted, wronged and wretched, full of pain;
Too full of bitter pain and shame to be

Akin to what so pains me, or estranged
From what it tortures me so much to lose.
O surely I am not, I cannot be
The thing that I begin to understand!

This is too wild and foolish. There are eight,
Twelve, fifteen, eighteen—eighteen, twenty grapes,
Twenty grapes on this cluster—twenty-one,
Twenty-one grapes that just begin to change.

But so was this unwilling—look at it,
This wretched leaf, this leaf that do I hold
Or does it cling to my unwilling hand
As clung the worm to its unwillingness?
To its unwillingness, to its, to mine,
To its unwilling helplessness and mine.
It is our helplessness and not our will.
No help by night, no remedy by day!
Only the worm is safe, that poisons us,
And makes us poison others, but not him.

Ours all the pain, the bitter grief, the shame,
'Tis we who suffer for it, we—the leaf,
And I—and Collatinus,—worst of all!
O worst of all that I must be the means,
That I—must, must—O mockery of will!
If I were willing should I suffer so?
There is no way—not if I die at once
Can he escape the poison and the pain.

Helpless. But why so helpless? Was this leaf
Less pure than any other, that the worm
Chose this one to crawl over and not that?
Why was this chosen to be so defiled?

If in itself, unknown unto itself,
Unknown and unsuspected, should have been
Something that fitted it to feed the worm!

Ha! the breeze blows it back to me again!
Off from my dress! I trample on it—So!

Be still, be still, be still! O but my brain
Is giddy with intruding thoughts that swarm
Like flies for carrion, and the very air
Quivers and murmurs with a hateful thought,
The merciless grasshoppers make me mad
With hissing all one word—O horrible,
That ever evil should give aught but pain!

I must be patient. What a day it is!
With its clear sky, its white unburthened clouds,
Its noiseless shadows and its glancing leaves,
Its songs, its voices and its easy wind
Charmed with the murmur of the moving trees!
O husband, love, where were you, ere the night
Made me your shame who used to be your praise!
No more, no more forever, never more!

MEDUSA.

ONE calm and cloudless winter night,
    Under a moonless sky—
Whence I had seen the gracious light
    Of sunset fade and die,—

I stood alone a little space,
    Where tree nor building bars
Its outlook, in a desert place,
    The best to see the stars.

No sound was in the frosty air,
    No light below the skies;
I looked above, and unaware
    Looked in Medusa's eyes;—

The eyes that neither laugh nor weep,
  That neither hope nor fear,
That neither watch nor dream nor sleep,
  Nor sympathize nor sneer;

The eyes that neither spurn nor choose,
  Nor question nor reply,
That neither pardon nor accuse,
  That yield not nor defy;

The eyes that hide not nor reveal,
  That trust not nor betray;
That acquiesce not nor appeal—
  The eyes that never pray.

O love that will not be forgot!
  O love that leaves alone!
O love that blinds and blesses not!
  O love that turns to stone!

A WINTER EVENING.

Expecting him, her fancy talks
(By like and unlike set astir)
Of one of her last summer walks
To where he sat expecting her.

WE had no sunset here to-day,
   Nor are there any stars to-night;
But all above was pearly gray
   And all beneath was silver white;
And still the snow-flakes fall and fall
   In silence, for the weary breeze
Is sleeping, and no noise at all
   Is in the bushes or the trees,
On which the snow lies like white moss,
   Too light to bend them; but the grass
Must be quite hidden all across

A WINTER EVENING.

The meadow through which he will pass
Unheard, unseen, till he is near
  The lilac sparkling in the glow
Of this my little lamp, placed here
  To call him to me through the snow.

'Tis not so very cold without;
  But here within 'tis light and warm,
The hot wood murmurs, wrapped about
  By lithe long flames of fickle form;
And swiftly running on, to make
  Its lurking cuckoo leap and laugh,
The clock's incessant chatterings wake
  An answering echo in behalf
Of sweeter noises than its own:
  Till, hearing them, I seem to see
Once more the meadows overgrown
  With waving grass, and every tree
With bright green leaves well woven close
  To take the sunlight, and the wind

Almost to take, that comes and goes
   And never quite makes up its mind.
And in the meadows near and far,
   With daisies and snapdragon dight,
Unanswerable crickets are
   Forever singing out of sight;
And little flickering brooks that flow
   To their own music ever, make
For me a music that I know—
   How well indeed, who used to take
The path so often close beside
   The brightest of them, singing past
Well-watered grass on either side,
   Till, o'er the little bridge at last,
Good-by to brook and path, but not
   Till, spite of all the surly bees
That grudge the treasure, I have got
   As many ear-drops as I please:
And then the meadow ('twas a sin
   To flout the quiet daisies so),

With scared grasshoppers out and in
  The grasses leaping as I go;
Along the moss-grown shaky wall,
  Across the close-nipped pasture-ground
Where only mulleins dare grow tall,
  And blackberry vines creep close around
The gray-green mossy rocks that sleep
  Luxurious in the flattering light
Of sunshine all day long, and keep
  Warm sides to feel of in the night;
Past patient cows that mildly gaze
  Upon me as I pass them by,
And stop to fix a lock that strays,
  And startle at a far-off cry;—
And then a turn, and there is naught
  Between me and the place I know
But vines and bushes interwrought
  To make a screening tangle go
About a green and golden glade,
  Where 'neath the appointed chestnut tree,

And quaintly dappled by its shade,
   Who is it I have come to see?
And yet, forsooth, the eager eyes
   Must cloud a little and go astray
A moment with the thoughts that rise
   Of many things, and will have way,
Before I dare to draw the screen
   Of interwoven leaves apart
A little way, and peer between,
   And see him, with as full a heart—

As now I have to see him there,
   Behind my lilac in the snow
Peering at me, and with an air
   As if a woman would not know!

A SPRING MORNING.

WHO would have thought that she could be so cold—
So cold and hard, and deaf and dumb and blind?
Oh she, whom it was summer to behold
In midst of winter! when the excluded wind
Stirred snow instead of flowers, and under ice
The brook went blindly, and the boughs were dumb
Of song and whisper, and no butterflies
Gleamed in the sunlight, and no bees were come,
Then she was warmth and colour and sweet song,
And life and light and loveliness—Alas!
And now when snows are melted, and ere long
All she prefigured will have come to pass,
Now she herself is colder than the snow
Is cold, is dead—Oh, how can she be so!

SHADOWS.

How good it is to see once more
   Green grasses turning gray before
The wilful blowing of the breeze;
And here and there from clouds and trees,
Over the moving meadow, slow
The changing shadows glide and go!

How good it is! but as before,
No summer breezes any more
Shall blow about her wayward hair;
Nor any summer meadows wear
Her passing shadow, passed away
With half the brightness of the day.

A CHANGE.

H E said, "Dew wets
No dearer flowers
Than violets:
Thro' long Spring hours
The wandering bees
Prove all, and meet
No flowers so sweet."

I planted these,
Whose perfumed bloom,
I thought would please;
And he, for whom
I bade them grow,—
Loves roses now!

A CHANGE.

God pity me!
I cannot see
  The end of pain.
The flowers I know
  Bloom not in vain,
Since Thou wilt care
To find them fair:
But Thou art—where?
  Faith falters so
When Love grows dim,
And 'twas for him
  I bade them grow!

AD FINEM.

I WOULD not have believed it then,
If any one had told me so—
Ere you shall see his face again
A year and more shall go.

And let them come again to-day
To pity me and prophesy,
And I will face them all and say
To all of them, You lie!

False prophets all, you lie, you lie!
I will believe no word but his;
Will say December is July,
That Autumn April is,

Rather than say he has forgot,
    Or will not come who bade me wait,
Who wait him and accuse him not
    Of being very late.

He said that he would come in Spring,
    And I believed—believe him now,
Though all the birds have ceased to sing
    And bare is every bough;

For Spring is not till he appear,
    Winter is not when he is nigh—
The only Lord of all my year,
    For whom I live—and die!

THE NEW NARCISSUS.

GIVEN up for all the unprofitable day,
  O'er the ship's side that moves not in her place,
To lean and look and languidly to trace
On the slow glass of the receding bay
The troubled image of a troubled face;
Or, with vague longing up and down to pace
The narrow deck, and of the far-away
Swift ships that glisten with momentary spray
Ask what avails a little larger space
Of insufficient ocean,—this is he
Whose stranded life, too careful to be free,
No dreams deliver, and all thoughts betray
To hate the calm that holds him in delay,
To doubt the wind that calls him to the sea.

A QUESTION.

1

BRIGHT buds that will not blow,
    Blown flowers that are not sweet,
    Fruits that no man can eat,
Sown seeds that will not grow,
    All men may meet.

2

Fair fields of fertile land
    Neglected utterly,
    Weeds where good grain should be,
Long stretches of ploughed sand,
    All men may see.

3.

Springs nauseous to the taste,
   Rills tangled in the grass,
   Wells breathing deadly gas,
Rivers that split and waste,
   All men may pass.

4.

Words—vain and idle words
   That vex the eager ear—
   No more what they appear
Than blown leaves are like birds,
   All men may hear.

5.

Paths circling in a maze,
   Clews sure to break or bind,
   Torches that burn and blind,
Guides that know not the ways,
   All men may find.

A QUESTION.

6.

Ambitions made to fall,
   Hopes swift to come and go,
   Dumb loves that chill like snow,
And friendships that enthrall,
   All men may know.

7.

Brief glimpses of faint joys
   Between long clouds of pain,
   Weak virtues that restrain,
And knowledge that annoys,
   All men may gain.

8.

But why with such as these,
   Men choose day after day
   To waste lives that they may
Make fruitful if they please
   What man can say?

PILGRIMAGE.

I. Setting Out.

SHE is so lovely that I long
　　With all my soul to sing one song
Before her, or at least to see
How heavenly fair the face must be
Of her, whom having never seen,
I long for and have called my Queen.

I go to seek her. Yes, to-day
Shall be the last of my delay:
I go to seek her, journeying through
Strange ways and wilds beloved of few,
But I must see her face before
My days for wandering are o'er.

And Youth is passing. Ah! my friend,
Too soon the sunlit days will end;
Too soon the uninspiring night
Will find me needing other light
Than lights their life who will not gain
The pain of joy, the joy of pain;

For of one thing my soul is sure—
There is no joy that can endure
Which is not grown of pain indeed.
So I plant pain, and from that seed
Wait hopeful ere the end to gain
True joy, the flower of real pain.

True joy which will endure—you say;—
"What is it after many a day
Of painful toil, if you shall gain
A moment's joy for days of pain—
A little glimpse of her, and then
The loneliness and dark again?"

But is it so? Look up—behold!
How all the westward clouds in gold
And crimson beauty take the light!
And tho' in half an hour the night
Will steal it from me, still would I
Walk miles and miles to see that sky.

And shall I not walk miles and miles
Just once to see her when she smiles?
Though she no more belong to me
When smiling than that sky I see,
Which yet seems somehow to shed down
A joy which makes its gold my own?

And it is mine! Upon my face
And in my heart I wear its grace
So surely, that if now to-night
All sunsets end, yet there is light
Enough left in my life, I know,
To set the darkness all aglow.

There is the reason! if that sky
Has such a power to beautify
My life that it may after thence
Give beautifying influence,
What may my life not hope to be
If Beauty's self should shine on me?

And so I go. The pain is long?
And brief the joy? There you are wrong;
For perfect joy can not be brief—
Joy is immortal; but for grief
Death lies in wait, and it shall die—
But joy has all eternity.

Ah! I am glad, for grief shall die,
And I shall see true joy—even I
Shall see it and it shall be mine;
And yours, my friend, for that divine
Full light of life if one man find
Is found indeed for all mankind.

And so I go. For me and you
And all the world I seek that true
Full light of joy, whose dwelling-place
Is in one undiscovered face
Whose smile shall to my soul supply
A life-long light to journey by,

Which I shall see: 'tis but to make
My life a journey for her sake,
To follow where the longings lead,
And with no guide but them succeed
In proving how well spent they were,
The days I lost in seeking her;

And, as it may be, by the way
If I sink wearily some day,
When most I need it I may see
The smiling face bent over me
A moment, and then it is gone,
And I walk on and on alone.

PILGRIMAGE.

And not alone; the wished-for smile
Shall keep me company the while,
Charm me from harm, draw me away
From all desire to stop or stray,
And make me bolder to aspire
By adding memory to desire.

And if not—still I go, I go!
The hope shall be enough, I know,
To save my life from being quite
Devoid of loveliness and light;
It is enough for me if I
Am still pursuing when I die.

And so I go. Would God, my friend,
That you were with me to the end!
But if at last, and far away
From where we separate to-day,
We meet each other face to face,
It will not seem a strange embrace.

II. Half Way.

1.

Has the bitterness found you?
Ah! foolish to deem,
While the hills yet surround you
And hold you and bound you,
   That this was your dream.

2.

From the fields that lie yonder
   It gleamed all aglow
With fresh beauty and wonder,
Which seem passing under
   Strange darknesses now:

3.

For you linger, mistaking

　The place where you stand

For the glory, that breaking

All o'er it, was making

　It worth your demand;

4.

Not the place, whose use ended

　As soon as 'twas won,

Allured, but the splendid

Glad light that ascended

　Inviting you on.

5.

On then! with the Spirit

　Most restless in rest

That guides who revere it,

And tortures who fear it

　And hold it supprest;

6.

Unsatisfied ever
But cheerful to strive,
Too wise to dissever
Joy from the endeavour
That keeps it alive;

7.

Still seeking and learning
And seeking anew,
Still winning and spurning,
Upborne by the yearning
That bids it pursue;

8.

What place shall restrain it
From always to range?
It strives but to gain it,
Outgrow and disdain it,
Most constant to change.

9.

Withhold it from ranging,
And what do you win?
Your own soul estranging,
And outer strife changing
For discord within!

10.

And who can restore you
The light you have lost,
While the shadows lie o'er you
Of hills yet before you
That wait to be crost?

11.

From the shadows that harm you,
Climb, loving the light
Which still shines to charm you
And gladden and warm you
And guide you aright;

12.

Only past hopes are hollow;
　The real remain,
And swift-winged as the swallow
Still call you to follow
　With longing again—

13.

Each something supplying,
　Lest any despond,
Each something denying,
And all testifying
　To something beyond.

III. Before the Gates.

Too long I wander lonely to and fro.
  O loved and loving, whom I have not seen,
  Declare yourself, and be indeed my Queen—
To rule and lead me where I long to go.
For now too weary, and almost in vain,
  Striving to keep the old smile on my face,
And make the joy of others cure my pain,
  I listen for you in the lonely place,
Which grows more lonely as day after day
  Too swiftly leaves me with my wish denied;
While hither, from within the gates, there stray
Sweet words and laughters—not so sweet as those
Which I still dream of, where the gates unclose,
  And we too enter gladly, side by side.

SIR GAWAINE'S LOVE.

" Me lust not of the caf ne of the stree,
Makè so long a tale as of the corn."

GUINEVERE.

LET me have all the story from yourself.
Was she indeed so ugly as they say—
She whom I know is now so beautiful?

GAWAINE.

Is she not beautiful?—so beautiful
That I dare even look upon your face,
And turn from that to look on hers again
And still say it is beautiful!

GUINEVERE.

      Nay, nay!
You make your praise too serious a thing,

With that so grave and earnest voice of yours,
For one to take it without afterthought
Of one's own worthiness—tell me of her;
How could you take her, Gawaine ? 'Tis a tale !

Gawaine.

How could I take her! Is she not most fair?
And yet to me it sometimes seems a dream
From which I dread to wake. But it is true.

Guinevere.

Why so it is—that she is beautiful.
But was she otherwise, or if she was,
How could you ever take her, still I say.

Gawaine.

To serve the king. Why, what else could I do?
You know how the king met her and from her—
The meanest creature in the world she seemed,
And yet the one of whom he had most need,

Without whose love his kingdom could not stand—
Learned the one way to overcome his foe;
And how—for all his kingdom was at stake,
And he was kingly in his gratitude—
He promised her that she should ask and have
Her dearest wish, and how she said at once:
'This is my dearest and my only wish,
That one of Arthur's knights shall marry me.'

GUINEVERE.

Too dear a wish for such a one as she!

GAWAINE.

So he thought, looking sidewise at her face—
A face in which no grace nor goodness showed.
But nothing else could tempt her; she had wished
And he had promised—let him keep his word.
So he rode back with a most heavy heart
To find himself entrapped a second time,
And would not speak at first; but afterward

To me, still seeking to find out his grief,
That I might somehow help him if I could,
Told what had happened, and more than he
   ought
Reproached himself. Well, it seemed hard at
   first,
And strange enough. But what else could I do?
I saw no other way and told him so—
My life was his—

          GUINEVERE.

              O, there it is again!
I cannot understand it. Men may die,
And so give all their lives, but—Gawaine, no!
There is no one before his death so cold
That he is not devoted to some hope—
Some self-tormenting, secret, sleepless hope—
To which he still clings closer as the years,
The barren, lonely years too swiftly go,
And leave him looking still to find his life—

His life, his own life, his true, real life,
Which still escapes him, and still more and more
Is longed for, as still more and more the years
Go from him unenjoyed, and steal away
The precious future, so made less and less,
And dearer as it lessens. Speak the truth!
How can one who has waited so to live—
So much life lost, so little left to him,
And yet that little holding all his life,
All that can justify the fruitless past
And save from utter blankness all the years—
How can one give away that hope of life?

GAWAINE.

He cannot, Guinevere, he never does;
And yet I know, I know! Yes, and will say
What I had thought before to leave unsaid;
But all is over now, both doubt and deed,
And you can understand me why I speak.—
How long ago it seems, two days ago!

A day to be remembered for itself,
A bright Spring day, and all the earth was new
With growing grass and beautiful bright. leaves
And brighter skies and the swift flight of birds
Not swifter than their singing—what a day !
Which took me, charmed to follow, to itself,
And led me from the garden—where the rest
Welcomed the Spring with smiles and whispered
    words—
Beyond the palace to the wider fields,
Where overhead the sky was broad and deep,
And all the beauty of a sunlit world
Lay open to my senses and my soul.
And seeing beauty grow in everything,
And all things fairer because each was fair,
And glad to see it all, what wonder then
That I should think no less of my own life
Than that it also might be beautiful ?
And thinking thus I saw the sun go down,
And in the fulfilled brightness of the West

Seemed to behold the light of some great joy—
The proof and the reward of real life,
Which I should gain, not for myself alone,
But for myself and through me for the world.
So all my life, my waiting, and my hope
Seemed justified, and I could still wait on,
Trusting the hope that made me think and say:
Surely, no one who bravely longs to live,
And bravely works and waits for it, shall fail
To win his life from the reluctant years—
His life, of which joy surely shall be part.

So I stood thinking there, and with the thought
Uprose the old love of my life again,
More beautiful than ever—the old love
I never dared confess to any one,
And hardly to myself, so dear it was;
And so most fearful was I lest my soul,
Seeking too clearly to define its hope,
Should feel itself outgrown by its desire,

And darkened in the shadow of its dream.

But now—set face to face with such a sky,

While round me all the noises of the day

Ceased, save one long, low murmur of deep joy,

To me the highest hope seemed surest, as it is—

When lo! even as I said so, a dark shape

Between me and the gladness of the gold!

The King, dusty and travel-worn and sad—

The King, a messenger from her who knew

The very answer to my soul's desire;

But then we knew it not.

      'Tis hard to say

How much perhaps the habit, learned of old,

To do whatever work there was to do,

Unasking my own safety or desire,

Saved me from being overborne by doubt;

But without hesitation—nay, indeed,

Almost with eagerness—so cold a dread

Of lurking cowardice came over me—

I bade the King at once be of good cheer,

For was my life not his—all of my life?
So I said easily enough, why not?
Just as one suddenly waked up at night
Mechanically reaches for his sword,
And stands on guard and shudders afterward.
But as the words slipped from me and were gone,
They seemed to hang before me like a cloud,
Thick, black, impassable, through which no light
Of earth or heaven could find me any more.
And bitterer came after, for the King,
Touching unconsciously the wound that I
Kept hardly hidden from him, said at once,
'Better that I and all my Kingdom fail,
Than that your life be dwarfed in saving it.
Shall I, who know how hard it is to live—
Shall I keep you from living all your life?
Shall I, who know how even another's sin
Poisons the purest life, give you away
To mere infection, shutting out your youth

From all the quickening health and help of love
Which all men need, the noblest most of all?'

That was the painfullest, for every word,
Too apt an ally to my doubtful fear,
Struck me and stung me like so many sparks
Of biting fire upon the naked flesh.
Even now I feel them, and remember how
I shrank, and hastily, to hide my pain,
Said what I hardly know, for all the world
Seemed unsubstantial in the utter dark,
And there was nothing left for me to do
But cling in very loneliness of soul
To this one dreadful chance of doing well;
Lest, letting go my hold of that, the earth
Should slide from under me and I be lost.
For, yes! that was what saved me—to hold fast
To that true law of life, proved always sure,
But hard to prove though easy to believe,
That he lives best and makes most of his life

Who puts it to most use. Use is the life of life,
And who most uses it most saves his life.
There I was safe, and clinging fast to that
The cloud passed over me, strong to dismay
But not to conquer. Then I saw and knew
The meaning and the worth of what we seek;
'Tis not so much to enjoy as to desire.
Joy is a necessary part of life;
But the best joy, the surest, fertilest,
Is not that which allures us from without,
But that which springs and grows within our-
    selves—
The joy which we create within ourselves
And are ourselves the rulers of—not that
Which would rule over us, and make our souls
Mere restless slaves of fickle influence.
Was it a loss then for me to let go
The outer vague, uncertain dreams and hopes?
Since to lose them was but to find myself,
And give my soul its rightful place again

Of lordly rule, and be at last a man
Strong in myself without external aid,
And so sure of my life I need no more
Weigh nicely all its uses, but be free
To use it everywhere and every day,
As common as my sword, finding my work
The common work, my joy the joy of all,
And so beside my own possessing all,
With no dread now of being called upon
For painful sacrifice, because I gain
The glad indifference of heroic hearts,
Who prove all things and hold fast what is good.
Ah! how the sky grew clear, and from my eyes
The mists were blown abroad before that
    thought
As from a cheerful breeze, and all the stars
Came forth, gleamed clear, and in the stainless
    sky
Glided to music, and my soul was glad
With a new sense of freedom and a new

And dearer love of life, meant to be made
A sure succession of productive days,
An infinite pursuit, which, rightly urged,
Wins always, and can never be outworn.
But now I tire you.

GUINEVERE.

    No! you puzzle me.
But after sunset is there not the night?

GAWAINE.

And stars—did I not say the stars were out,
Supreme above the trouble of the clouds?
Forgive my boasting, but I half forget,
Thinking of her, the end that might have been.

GUINEVERE.

You are Gawaine, and I am Guinevere—
But tell me how it ended.

GAWAINE.

                    The next day
The King and Tristram, Launcelot and Kay,
And more, not many, with us, we rode forth
In the first freshness of the early morn
To where the King had met her—not in vain.
There is a place, apart from any way,
Hard by the forest, where an oak tree grows
Quite all alone, but that it overhangs
A single holly, and mid-way between
The oak, just won to put away at last
His barren doubt and from the genial Spring
Withhold no one of all his tender leaves,
And the low holly that all winter long
Can keep alive its strange suggestive green,
There she was sitting on the ground. Ah me!
It was too bitter to see such a thing
Blacken the brightness of the cheerful sky
And make the world a failure; and for this—
Was it for this I had reserved myself?

Foregone so much for this—for this so long
Borne with delay, and through the lonely years
Scorned not the lesson of their loneliness?
A bitter fruit to gather at the last!
I think I must have shown it in my face
More than I should, the pain that took me then
As I stood motionless, with eyes withdrawn
From all the world but that which made it sad;
For all at once I heard, as if it were
The fatal echo of my speechless thought,
The voice of Launcelot, that said, *Alas!*
And at the words, so full of piteous love,
My heart was softened to remember now
The knighthood that I boasted, and my eyes
Made clear to see how much more want there was
Of love and pity in this wretched one,
From whom, because hers was so great a need,
Men turned away and could not pity her.
And by what right, I could but ask myself—
By what right was this woman quite cut off

From any touch of kindly human hands,
Quite thrust apart from all mankind, to whom,
However base, she was more near akin
Than to the gracious sunlight and the breeze,
That had no more of scorn nor less of love
For her than for another? By what right
Was she unlovely? And why could I not
Avoid a sense of shame, unfelt before,
That made me guilty of her wretchedness,
As each by each the questions that I asked
Were sternly left unanswered? From that time
I knew that over all my life henceforth
She had a power. And, shall I tell you all?—
I know not why, but I was glad of it;
And irresistibly drawn down at once
To look upon her face, at once I saw
(This is a strange thing that I tell you of)—
But looking down I saw within her eyes
The same desire that lived within my own,
But much more patient, as if more secure,

A long desire that questioned all it saw,
That questioned me with a prevailing look,
As if in judgment of me; or again,
As if imploring me as much or more
For my sake than for hers, to let my heart
Not close itself against the eager wish
Which seized me suddenly, with more of love
Than pity of her, to stoop swiftly down
And lift and kiss her quickly on the mouth!

(A voice from the hall, singing.)

After the fight!
Then let Love look upon me,
When I am proved a knight
Worthy to bear the sight
Of her whose love has won me—
Then let Love look upon me,
After the fight!

GAWAINE.

Launcelot's song—what a glad voice he has!

(From the hall.)
After the fight!
Then let me be rewarded,
  When I am proved a knight
  Worthy to wear aright
  Her favour bravely guarded—
Then let me be rewarded,
  After the fight!

GUINEVERE.

And you proved knight who fought so well for
  her;
You too are well rewarded, are you not?
And there she is—see, in the garden now.
And you can no more now resist her eyes
Than on that morning. Well, then, you shall go.
Thanks for so glad a story.

(Gawaine goes out.)

Would there were
Some one in all the world to kiss me so—
If only Launcelot were also saved!

HER NAME.

I THINK her true name must be Marguerite,
So bright she is and so serenely sweet,
This girl I never spoke to; and have seen
Twice, and twice only; once as o'er the green
She walked to church, and once just now as she
Met and passed by, and never thought of me,
Who smiled to think how all the dusty street
Seemed like fresh fields, and murmured Marguerite!

IN WINTER.

WHAT will you give? you seem to ask, and I
What can I give you? answer, and am sad;
For what is left of lovely that I had?
Or what of sweet will not the days deny
To let me gain and give you by-and-bye?
O Love! O Love! what was it that forbade
To ask of me while yet I could be glad
To hear you ask it, and to make reply?
For Spring was warm, and Summer all aglow,
Autumn not cold, and not too quick to tire;
But of the Winter if you will inquire,
What can it do for you but sigh and show,
Still rustling faintly over so much snow,
The ungathered flowers of my too long desire?

GREENHOUSE FLOWERS.

'TIS too late to find her flowers
　　Such as I should rather give—
Such as sad and sunlit hours
　　Equally have taught to live.

　　How can these, that never guessed
　　　　How the evil helps the good—
　　How can these to her suggest
　　　　Aught of what I wish they could?

　　How can these that never felt
　　　　Doubt and fear and hope deferred,
　　Ere the snows began to melt,
　　　　Ere the frozen earth was stirred;

How can these that never thrilled
    In the midst of their distress,
With the hope of hope fulfilled—
    How can these my thought express?

Yet, because perhaps they may
    Please her once or twice to see,
Let them go and have their day,
    Happier than they ought to be!

TILL SPRING.

IN frozen earth,
    Beneath the snow,
  A wondrous birth
  Is lurking now;

I lay my ear
    Against the ground,
I cannot hear
    The slightest sound.

No sound is heard;
    The hard and bare
Earth is not stirred,
    Yet they are there;

TILL SPRING.

Not very far—
  Far under these
Cold snows they are,
  My crocuses!

Are there beneath
  The ice and snow,
And live and breathe,
  And feel and grow,

With a sublime
  Bélief in Fate—
They know their time,
  And can await,

Upgrowing still,
  Though still unheard
Or felt until
  The earth is stirred,

And opes, and lo!
   How slight a thing
Can shame the snow
   And prove the Spring!

I lay my ear
   Against the ground,
I cannot hear
   The slightest sound;

And yet, not far—
   Far under these
Cold snows, there are
   Warm crocuses.

Ah! little call
   Were there for doubt,
If flowers were all
   I cared about!

If every thing
  I think of were
Not swift to bring
  Me thoughts of her;

If while I say,
  Would March were o'er!
I did not pray
  For something more;

If while I watch
  The frozen ground,
And strive to catch
  Some little sound

Of life astir
  Beneath the frost,
'Twere not of her
  I think the most;

If while I say,
  Soon must the snows
Melt and make way,
  And let unclose

Sweet flowers that brood
  In secret now—
I only could
  Forget somehow,

Somehow forego
  The old demur,—
Will it be so
  With her, with her?

IN NUBIBUS.

THIS is a dream I had of her
When in the middle seas we were.

Sunlight possessed the clouds again,
Well emptied of unfruitful rain,
When, leaning o'er the vessel's side,
I watched the bubbles rise and glide
And break and pass away beneath;
And heard the creamy waters seethe,
As when an undecided breeze
Plays in the branches of the trees
Just ere the leaves begin to fall;
And as I listened, slowly all
The elm-tree branches on the Green
Rose up before me; and between
The stately trees on either side
I saw the pathway, smooth and wide,
In which I once had walked with her;

And in it men and women were,
Who came and went no otherwise
Than vague cloud-shadows to my eyes,
And whispering bubbles to my ear,
Who neither cared to see nor hear,
And straight forgot them every one.

But when the last of them was gone,
And now from end to end the walk
Was empty of them and their talk,
A listening, longing silence fell
Upon the elm-trees like a spell
Of expectation and desire,
And quick I saw the impulsive fire
Of sunset overflush the white
And waiting clouds with rosy light;
And then a breeze ran all along
The pathway, as if from a song—
Imparting freshness as it ran,
Till all the autumn leaves began

Mid-summer murmurs in the air,
And suddenly I saw her there—
And felt my heart leap up, and then
As suddenly shrink back again
To see that she was not alone;
But with her walking there was one
Whose face turned sidewise, as it were
The better so to hark to her,
Showed not enough to let me know
What man it was I envied so:
And yet I could not go away,
But fascinated still to stay,
And wait till they should pass me by,
I stood and watched them cloudily,
And saw them coming near and near,
And nearer yet, till I could hear
Her voice and recognize his face;
And, save that a transmitted grace
Made it not easy to be known,
So went the dream—it was my own.

A PAUSE.

TO have the imploring hands of her
    Clasped on his shoulder, and his cheek
Brushed over slowly by the stir
    Of thrilling hair, and not to speak;

To see within the unlifted eyes
    More than the fallen fringes prove
Enough to hide, to see the rise
    Of tear-drops in them, and not move;

Would this be strange? And yet at last,
    What weary man may not do this,
Seeing when the long pursuit is past,
    To only cease how sweet it is?

To only cease and be as one
    Who, when the fever leaves him, lies
Careless of what is come or gone,
    Which yet he cannot realize;

For all his little thought is spent
    In wondering what it was that gave
To be so quiet and content,
    While yet he is not in the grave.

TOO LATE.

Dreaming again, I dreamed she kissed me dead
Who would not kiss me living; not less cold
Grew the mute lips; nor could the wilful gold,
Brushing against them from the bended head,
Warm the wan cheeks to any show of red;
Nor could the touch of falling tears withhold
The heavy eyes from slumber, uncontrolled
By longing any longer; but, instead,
The sleepless soul she could not see to save
Stood close to her with eager envious eyes,
To see death rob him of the tardy prize,
And waste the precious kisses that she gave,
Only at last to prove at such a cost
How sweet is life to him whose life is lost!

AUTUMN SONG.

WHAT have rustling leaves to say,
    Fit to make us sad or glad?
Ere the wind blew us away,
    Much delight in life we had.

Now we both of us are sad,
    Both of us would death defer—
You, because you are not glad,
    We, because we always were.

This is what the brown leaves say,
    With a sadness less than mine:
Dear, if I should die to-day,
    Give me something to resign.

UNDERSONG.

WHILE I linger in her room,
    Singing idly at her feet,
Si douce est la Marguerite,
Are the clover blossoms sweet?
Are the apple-trees in bloom,
While I linger in her room?

Is there murmuring of bees
While I murmur at her feet,
Si douce est la Marguerite?
Is there singing swift and sweet
By the brook-side, in the trees?
Is there murmuring of bees?

In the springtime of the year,
Sitting singing at her feet,
Si douce est la Marguerite,
Is there then no other sweet
Thing to see or have or hear
In the springtime of the year?

A PRODIGAL.

THESE are the fields by which we went:
    Few flowers, if any, then there were;
The grasshoppers had almost spent
    Their singing when I walked with her;

The gold and crimson glow that was
    Among the woods was soon to die;
Dead leaves were on the failing grass,
    And no birds then to sing or fly:

"And let there be no flowers," I said,
    "And let the last leaf fade and fall!
When all their grace and charm are fled,
    What matter, since she has them all?

"What matter, since no song-bird gives
  Such pleasure as to hear her speak,
Since in no flower the colour lives
  So pure and sure as in her cheek?

"Since not the calmest lake receives
  From bird or flower a lovelier fleck
Of shadow than her ear-ring leaves
  Upon the whiteness of her neck?

"Since all the stir of rustling trees,
  Or waving grass, to me is less
Than to be near her when the breeze
  Plays with her hair and with her dress?

"Since all that I have seen or sought
  Or hoped or dreamed I find at last
In her harmoniously enwrought,
  And by a special charm surpassed?"

A PRODIGAL.

The last leaf took not long to fall,
   The last flower faded long ago,
The grass cannot be seen at all,
   Quite overfallen with frozen snow;

Only the breeze that blew her dress
   Seems still the same as on that day;
As then, so it is now no less
   The voice of all I cannot say:

As then its murmur did not fail
   All my unthrifty hope to share,
So now with its most lonely wail
   How well it echoes my despair!

MAGGIOR DOLORE.

FORGIVE you? Yes, why not?
   Forget you? Would I could,
   With all the rest that should
But will not be forgot!

The longings that outlive
   The hopes that you have slain;
   All that I could not gain,
And all you would not give.

But you have given me quite
   Too much, whose hands withhold
   None of the gloom and cold—
But all the sleep of night;

Of night that sees aghast
  How few things to regret,
  How many to forget
The barren days amassed:

For what is worse than this—
  Than to have never had
  The joy that makes men sad
To know how brief it is?

Than to have never known
  The one delight well worth
  A man's grief in the earth
When it is overgrown?

Than to be forced to choose
  The grief without the cause —
  Than to lament not loss,
But want of what to lose?

Than to be one who is
   Forbidden of Love to dwell
   In either Heaven or Hell—
What can be worse than this?

Ah! it were not too hard,
   If you had let me live,
   To bless you, not forgive,
Whate'er were afterward;

To say, and say it glad,—
   Because you loved before,
   Do this to me, and more!
To lose is to have had.

GONE.

WHY have they lighted
   The empty room?
Since she has left it,
   Black night and gloom
Should have it wholly—
   Its walls, its floor,
Its lifeless window,
   Its useless door.

I stand without it
   And see, alas!
Too much, too little
   Of all that was;
Her books, her pictures,
   Her empty chair—
O, hide them from me!
   She is not there.

Draw close the curtains,
　Put out the light;
Let darkness enter
　And have from sight
What once was precious
　And now is vain—
Once full of pleasure
　And now of pain!

Draw close and cover
　The cheat, the change,
The sweet grown bitter,
　The dear things strange;
With such a darkness
　As is in me,
Conceal and cover
　The mockery!

THE MORAL.

THE play is ended? Be it so!
  What use to criticise?
And yet, perhaps 'twere well to know
  What moral underlies.

For, as I read it, it is such
  As both may ponder o'er;
Had I not loved you quite so much,
  You might have loved me more.

THE END.

THE sweetest songs are those
    That few men ever hear
And no men ever sing;

The clearest skies are those
    That furthest off appear
To birds of strongest wing;

The dearest loves are those
    That no man can come near
With his best following.

PART SECOND.

WITH NATURE.

VITA VITALIS.

I.

WHEN first the Spring grasses
    Take motion, and glisten
In sun-litten masses,
Wherethrough the brook passes
    And shimmers and sings;
When first the birds woo me
    To linger and listen,
And watch them upspringing
    On wonderful wings;
When breezes are bringing
Sweet scents to renew me,
Sweet sounds thrilling through me,
    From apple blooms over
    The blossoming clover,
Where bees murmur, clinging

With passionate pleasure,
   And butterflies wander
In silence, at leisure,
   Like spirits that ponder
Inscrutable things;—

Then always and ever,
Despite my endeavour
   To 'scape its control,
Some inflowing sadness
Discolours the gladness
   That freshens my soul;
Some answerless question,
Some subtile suggestion,
   Some shyly returning
Unsought recollection;
Some eager projection
   Of vague undiscerning,
   But passionate yearning;
A hoping, regretting,

Remembering, forgetting;
A groping, a reaching,
Demanding, beseeching;
A strangeness, a dearness,
A distance, a nearness;
Perplexes, excites me,
Repels me, invites me
   And fills me with fear:

With fear of foregoing
My life without knowing
   The life that without me,
   Above me, about me,
Is ceaselessly flowing
   So near me, so near!—
So near, and yet ever
Beyond my endeavour
To woo it and win it,
To have it and be it,
To lose myself in it.

I only can see it,
And feel it and hear it,
And love it and fear it,
   So willing to bless me,
   So stern to repress me.
What is it—what is it
Which makes me to miss it,
And only to miss it?
   What charm to be spoken?
   What spell to be broken,
Before I regain it
Once more, or attain it
At last, and inherit
   And hold as securely
As any of these,
The life that my spirit
   Remembers obscurely,
Obscurely foresees?

II.

Winged spirits, that wander
In silence and ponder
  Inscrutable things,
Ah! why do ye shun me?
Float over, light on me,
O touch me and thrill me,
With watchfulness fill me!
Nay! fan me and still me,
  Ye wonderful wings,
To slumber, if only,
Me sleeping, my lonely
  Shy spirit, who knew you
  Once haply, can woo you
  To take her unto you
Once more where ye wander
In silence and ponder
  Inscrutable things!

A DAY.

1.

WHERE but few feet ever stray,
   Far beyond the path's advances,
All alone an idler lay
Half a breezy summer day
   Underneath a chestnut's branches;

2.

Not a stranger to the place,
   For the daisies nodded to him,
And the grass in lines of grace
Bending over, touched his face
   With light kisses thrilling through him.

3.

Close beside his harmless hand
  Swinging bees would suck the clover,
And a moment to be scanned
Sunlit butterflies expand
  Easy wings to bear them over.

4.

All about him, full of glee,
  Careless cricket-songs were ringing,
And the wild birds in the tree
Settled down where he could see
  While he heard them gayly singing.

5.

Overhead he saw the trees
  Nod and beckon to each other,
And, too glad to be at ease,
Saw the green leaves in the breeze
  Tingle touching one another;

6.

Saw the little lonely rill
 In a line of greener growing,
Slipping downward from the hill,
Curving here and there at will,
 Through the tangled grasses going;

7.

Saw the play about his feet
 Of the flickering light and shadow;
Saw the sunlight go to meet
Glancing corn and waving wheat;
 Saw the mowers in the meadow;

8.

Saw the waves leap up and play
 On the palpitating river,
Flowing out to find the bay,
And the white ships far away
 Sailing on and on forever;

9.

Saw the hills upon whose side
   Slow cloud-shadows love to dally;
Saw the high hills, with the pride
Of dark forests belted wide,
   Over many a misty valley;

10.

Saw far-off the thin and steep
   Cloudy mountain-lands of wonder,
Where unseen the torrents leap
Over rifted rocks that keep
   Echoing memories of the thunder;

11.

Saw the self-supporting sky
   Ever more and more receding;
Loth to linger, loth to fly,
Saw the clouds go floating by,
   Stranger shapes to strange succeeding;

12.

Saw and mused and went away,
   Whether light or heavy hearted,
It were hard for him to say,
For a something came that day
   And a something had departed;

13.

And his soul was overfraught
   With a passion e'er returning;
With the pain that comes unsought
Of unutterable thought,
   And the restlessness of yearning.

THE RIVER.

Day after day
   I see the sunlit river
Float slowly on its way
   Thro' pleasant fields that never
Can charm it to delay,
Day after day.

Day after day
   It thrills as on its bosom
The shifting shadows play
   Of leaf, and bud, and blossom,
But still keeps on its way
Day after day.

Day after day
    It answers with its singing
Blithe birds and crickets gay,
    And smiles on breezes bringing
Sweet scents from far away,
Day after day.

Day after day
    "Sweet is it to have found you,"
It sings; "but far away,
    And farther yet beyond you,
I flow to find the bay
Day after day."

Day after day,
    "Why should my going grieve you?"
It sings; "O, you who may,
    Come with me or I leave you,"
Still flowing to the bay
Day after day.

"IN THE SPRING-TIME."

SEE what I saw to-day,
  Just as I turned away
To leave the budding wood,
And paused and understood
The meaning of Spring weather;
Two lovers close together,
That,—where at last the laughing brook
Glides to the lake,—with dreamy look
And lips half-parted in a smile—
Stood charmed to watch a little isle,
Past which the waves went rippling on
With softer music to the swan
That sat there in enchanted rest,
Unmoving on her nest.

IN EARLY APRIL.

THE cold is over, the snows are gone,
    The grass begins to be green once more,
And shyly opening one by one,
    The crocuses blossom beside the door;
    Love, if you love me, love me more!

The tops of the maples are faintly red,
    The amber willows are seen afar;
And laughing, chirruping overhead,
    The birds that glisten, how glad they are!
    Dearest, the nearest is still too far!

IN MAY.

Now that the green hill-side has quite
　　Forgot that it was ever white,
With quivering grasses clothed upon;
And dandelions invite the sun;
And columbines have found a way
To overcome the hard and gray
Old rocks that also feel the Spring;
And birds make love and swing and sing
On boughs which were so bare of late;
And bees become importunate;
And butterflies are quite at ease
Upon the well-contented breeze,
Which only is enough to make
A shadowy laughter on the lake;

And all the clouds, that here and there
Are floating, melting in the air,
Are such as beautify the blue;—
Now what is worthier, May, than you
Of all my praise, of all my love,
Except whom you remind me of?

SPRING SONG.

1.

MORE soft and white and light,
    More fragrant than the snow,
The cherry flowers are falling
And floating to and fro
About the happy trees;
And happy birds are calling
Each other, and the breeze
Is listening, loth to go.

2.

And yet these are the trees
That seemed so cold and stern
To winter's warmest weather;
Wait till it is my turn—

Wait till the good days bring
My love and me together,
Breezes, and I will sing
Songs you would love to learn!

3.

Till then I too, like you,
In a bewildered quest,
Too vainly praying ever
Wholly to be possest,
Am neither free nor thrall;
In all things something, never
In one thing finding all;
Unanswered and unblest.

MAY SONG.

THERE is grass now where the snow was
    Everywhere;
There are blossoms now for snow-flakes
    In the air;
And the birds have hiding-places
    In the trees,
Where the green leaves turn and tremble
    To the breeze;
And where the ice was, now the swan
Moves the lake she floats upon.

O my Love! and there is singing
    Now to hear;
And a motion and a murmur
    Far and near,

In the grasses, in the waters,
      In the flowers,
Fill with mystery of music
      All the hours,
Made too delightful now for one
To dare to live his life alone.

Come then, come, my Love, and listen,
      Come and see!
Come and share the beauty with me;
      Come and be
Its interpreter to make it
      Understood,
Its enhancer, Love, to make it
      Doubly good;
Till I perhaps grow lovely too,
Thanks to the spring-time and to you!

MOONLIGHT IN MAY.

THANKS! for I understand you, happy trees!
   And smile with you at all that made me sad,
Drawn unawares beyond all griefs I had
Into the truthfulness of clear moonlight,
Before whose frankness I can banish quite
The old forlorn endeavour to be glad,
And carelessly stand listening as I please
To the low rustle on the sparkling shore
Of conscious waves, that, ripplingly at ease,
Outrun the light and lead it on before;
Or to the murmur of the moonlit trees,
Whom time of waiting and reserve is o'er,
Whom Spring has taught to captivate the breeze,
And charm the nights made musical once more.

IN THE MEADOW.

IDLE, and all in love with idleness;
Caught in the net-work that my oak-tree weaves
Of light and shadow with his thrilling leaves,
And charmed to hear his murmured songs no less,
On the shorn grass I lie, and let the excess
Of summer life seem only summer play;
Even to the farmers working far away,
Where one man lifts and strenuously heaves
A bristly haycock up to him who stands
Unsteadily upon the swaying load,
Which, while the shuffling oxen slowly pass,
Touched into wakefulness by voice and goad,
He shapes and smooths, and turning in his hands,
The long fork glistens like a rod of glass.

BY THE LAKE.

SEE how the restless melancholy lake
　Gives all itself, too vainly evermore,
　Up to the blankness of the barren shore
Which cannot answer it again, nor take
Warmth to its loveless life from lips that ache
　With kissing and beseeching o'er and o'er.
　O bitterness of life, not known before!
Who shall deliver it from loves that make
　No answer to its yearning, strangely strong
To shut it in and waste its noblest powers?
　Making a moan of what was meant for song,
And for its hope of growing grass and flowers,
　Condemning it to see its best endeavour
　End in slow foam on fruitless sands forever.

BY THE BAY.

ON the smooth shore I stand alone and see
    A wonder in the distance: there the bay,
Drawn on to meet and mingle far away
With the broad sky's unstained serenity,
Pauses at last from panting restlessly;
Smooths his short waves, and scorning to delay,
Falls from the rounded world with all his weight
In silence through the silences below;
Where nothing balks the aimless overflow,
Till all the solid waters separate,
Split into streams, that bursting as they go
Fly off in rain, that ends in scattered spray
And mist that rises for the winds to blow
Hither and thither in unending play.

THE MIST.

I SAW along the lifeless sea
A mist come creeping stealthily,
Without a noise and slow,
A crouching mist come crawling low
Along the lifeless sea.

None marked that creeping, crawling mist
That crawled along the sea,
That crept and crawled so stealthily
And was so weak and white;
The moon was shining clear, I wist,
Above it in the night.

I saw it creeping, crawling low,
Slow crawling from the sea,
I saw it creep and crawl and grow
Till all the stifled earth below
Was shrouded silently :

I saw it creep and crawl and grow,
A forceless, formless thing,
Determined, tireless, ceaseless, slow,
Silent and silencing;
I saw it creep and crawl and rise
And crawl into the skies;

The stars began to faint and fail,
That were so pure and clear;
The moon took on a loathsome look
Of likeness to her fear—
That closer crawled and clung to her
And clung more near and near.

THE MIST.

The smothered moon went out and left
Not even the mist to see,
Mere blankness, and a sickening sense
Of something worse to be;
And certainly in midst of it
An awful thing I wist,
It was to know that all the world
Was nothing but a mist,
But a creeping, crawling mist.

RARA AVIS.

STANDING in shade, beside a path that lay
Full in the sunlight of the afternoon,
A gush of song from some bird far away
I heard arise and sink again as soon;

And still I listened, but no more I heard,
And all I saw was on the sunny ground
The flying shadow of an unseen bird,
No sooner come, than gone without a sound.

And so a song that I have never heard
Surpasses all that I shall ever hear,
And by the shadow of a vanished bird
The rest are darkened and not very dear.

THE KATYDID.

WHO knows of what the katydid
Sings every night where he is hid
In secret grasses or in trees
That have so many mysteries?
But under faint far stars, that peer
Through fainter clouds, I stand and hear
Him singing, and know not indeed
If any other song I need;
If any other song there be
So full of thrilling things to me;
Deluding me with old delights
That wake and make less happy nights
Not wholly barren for their sakes;
And old and new desires it wakes

For sweeter things than are; and all
That ever was or is or shall
Be made for longing or regret
It mingles and makes lovelier yet;
Till now if over or below
He sing or cease I hardly know!

A VINE.

ROOTED and sure to grow
   Serenely in poor places,
It lets its freshness flow
   O'er barren rocks, and graces
Their blankness till they show,
With green and crimson glow,
   As if themselves did make
   The beauty that they take.

This is the true man's way;
   To let no kind of chances
Warp him or turn astray;
   The blankest circumstances
Shall give his spirit play
If he will—as he may—
   Because the rest are slow,
   Strive all the more to grow.

ON THE BEACH.

THANKS to the few fair clouds that show
    So white against the blue,
At last even I begin to know
    What I was born to do;

What else but here alone to lie
    And bask me in the sun?
Well pleased to see the sails go by
    In silence one by one;

Or lovingly, along the low
    Smooth shore no plough depraves,
To watch the long low lazy flow
    Of the luxurious waves.

A GLIMPSE OF LIFE.

OH, not in vain some happier influence led
My feet to wander where few footsteps go!
After so long a pacing to and fro
In barren ways, how good it is instead,
Here where the blue is ample overhead,
And where the green is plentiful below,
To be alone and let the unquestioned flow
Of real life control me quieted!
Quieted, yes! and brought near to behold
The only life that makes me loth to die;
Whether the grass or whether the light breeze
Gladden me more, or whether it be these
Slim silver birches, lifting to the sky
Such quivering fountains of sunshiny gold.

MY STAR.

THAT is my star, that single one,
    Who, rising first and all alone
Ere yet the day is fairly gone,

Pale with old love and new delight,
Stands thrilling on the lonely height,
Prophet and herald of the night;

Whom many more shall greet, but none
So grandly as this lonely one.

MAN AND NATURE.

O STEADFAST trees, that know
  Rain, hail and sleet and snow,
And all the winds that blow;
  But when spring comes, can then
  So freshly bud again
Forgetful of the wrong!

Waters that deep below
The stubborn ice can go
With quiet underflow;
  Contented to be dumb
  Till spring herself shall come
To listen to your song!

Stars that the clouds pass o'er
And stain not, but make more
Alluring than before ;—
  How good it is for us
  That your lives are not thus
Prevented, but made strong !

CALM AND COLD.

BREAK into spray, and fly and fill the air
With ghastly mist that freezes ere it falls,
O struggling waves! whom not the wind appals,
Nor all the wrestling tempests overbear,
But secret fear, lest, pausing weary there,
Instead of peace, renewing whom it calls,
The subtle cold, that levels and enthralls,
Should creep and find and bind you unaware:
And what were worse than, smoothly calm and
    cold,
Wrapt in false peace, to fancy strife is o'er,
Forget the woes that all the winds deplore,
Forget the cares that all the clouds enfold,
Watch not nor wait for changes as of old,
And feel the movement of the world no more!

WINTER SUNRISE.

WHEN I consider, as I am forced to do,
    The many causes of my discontent,
And count my failures, and remember too
How many hopes the failures represent;
The hope of seeing what I have not seen,
The hope of winning what I have not won,
The hope of being what I have not been,
The hope of doing what I have not done;
When I remember and consider these—
Against my Past my Present seems to lie
As bare and black as yonder barren trees
Against the brightness of the morning sky,
Whose golden expectation puts to shame
The lurking hopes to which they still lay claim.

WINTER SUNSET.

I SAW a cloud at set of sun
   Exceeding white and fair,
High over every other one,
   And poised in purer air;

Like one that follows, forward bent,
   With arms outspread before,
Into the splendid west he went
   Just as the ·day was o'er;

I saw him turn to rosy red,
   I saw him turn to fire,
I saw him burn away instead
   Of ceasing to desire.

BY THE FIRESIDE.

(December 26.)

SAFELY at home, what is it that I hear
　　In the wind's moaning and the driven snow
That will not let me rest? Strange sounds of woe
From icy sailors battling with their fear;
The dreadful rush of shuddering ships that steer
For safety from the harbours that they know;
The thunder of blown icebergs as they go
Together in the darkness; and more near,
And worse than all the tumult of the seas,
A long low moan and sound of scanty tears
From hungry men and women as they freeze.
O Christ! the world is sad these many years
For many causes; would that one might cease
From making vain all promises of peace!

THE MEN OF CRETE.

(January, 1867.)

WOULD that death were as far removed as fear
From all heroic hearts! Shall death be known
The only friend of heroes left alone
To fight for what men say that they revere,
Unhelped, unheard? and dying shall they hear
Only a longer wail, a deeper moan
From all they love, more utterly o'erthrown
Because they loved, and proved their love sincere?
O men! how long shall this great wrong endure?
The slave be ruler, and the hero slave,
Truth's service suffering, and earth too poor
To give her noblemen more than a grave?
But take it, Cretans! for the tree is sure
Whose branches murmur o'er the martyred brave.

THE LION OF LUCERNE.

I.

SILENT it is, but over it the trees
And under it the waters, and around
The bees and birds and grasses make a sound
Of life whose movement is all grace and ease,
Devoid of fears, devoid of ecstasies,
But full of joy as careless as profound;
Silent it is, but none the less at last
Its mute insistence overcomes the ear
And steals the pleasure that it had to hear
Earth's peaceful noises, which seem changing fast
Into mere mockery, as the wave-like Past,
Recurring sullenly, brings near and near
The unjoyful murmur of man's ceaseless strife,
Let break in vain against the shore of life.

THE LION OF LUCERNE.

II.

YET there is life, and there is joy and peace;
Life before death, and peace this side the grave,
And joy in Earth, for this is what we crave,
Not to postpone, nor to forego and cease,
But in fulfilment to obtain release
From strife which vexes, but at last shall save:
Therefore to you, blithe singing birds and bees,
To you, soft trickling waters, and to you,
Slow melting cloud-wreaths in the unruffled blue,
Above the movement of the mingled trees,
To you once more my soul returns and sees,
And hears, not mockery, but a calm and true
Correction and approval of the strife,
Which is not life, but shall attain to life.

MY PLACE.

THERE are more reasons than I care to know
Why I should love this place of mine so well,
And not the least of them perhaps is this:
That never yet have I seen any one
Of those,—but few,—who even pass it by,
Who ever thought of loving it at all,
Or ever fancied, much less knew how near,
For me at least, it is to Paradise.

A place reserved, a place apart, afar
From any human love but only mine;
Yet in itself most lovely (as indeed
My love for it is quite enough to prove),
Though not another love it but myself,
Who therefore love it only all the more.

For who can say he knows what Nature is,
Till he have found him out some sacred spot
Where none delights to linger but himself?
But if he once has found him such a place,
O! there for him, wherever his foot fall,
As from the hoof of Pegasus, upsprings
A living Hippocrene, whereof his soul
May drink and be inspired for evermore.
But let him, as with dragons round about,
Shut in and keep his garden of delight,
Lest, if he find another foot-print there,
His fountain change into a lifeless pool,
Or shyly sink into the earth again.
Once in a great while one may take his friend
(For, if he be indeed a friend, the law
Of oneness is not too much disobeyed)
To see the place and yet preserve his love;—
But for the time he loses, I affirm,
The best of what its influence affords
To him alone who visits it alone;—

MY PLACE.

Just as one to a woman whom he loves
In an unselfish moment brings a friend,
But goes perforce to visit her alone
Whenever he would be supremely blest.

Hear something, therefore, now about my place.
But first, I will not tell you where it is,
Lest you should choose to go there for yourself,
And find it not so beautiful to you
As I say it is beautiful to me;
And after think as ill of me, perhaps,
As some unhappy moralists of those
Old painters who were not ashamed to make
Madonnas of their mistresses. Alas!

From the main road I turn abrupt, and walk,
Shadowed by lazy willows (of our trees
The first to show, the last to shed their leaves—
Most hopeful and most faithful of them all),
A little way along a lonely lane

Which leads me to the entrance of my place—
So I have named it—which, though often seen,
Yet somehow always takes me by surprise.

It seems to be a road—though never yet
Have I seen horse or wagon enter it—
Which passes downward crookedly between
Old rocks which overshadow it all day:
Old rocks whose tops are overgrown with grass,
Where violets delay dewdrops from the sun,
And dandelions show like midsummer stars,
Or languid moons at mid-day, ere the breeze
Has played the sower with them; daisies, too,
Contemplative till Fall; and in the Fall
Frank purple asters, and glad golden rod:
Slim birch trees shadow them not heavily,
And overlean the pass from either side,
With silver trunks and shining restless leaves,
And twigs so slight that when the leaves are
   gone

I scarce regret their absence in the Fall,
So delicately beautiful appear
The loosely interwoven, sharp, thin lines,
With pendulous seed-tassels held aloft
In shifting tracery on the pale blue sky.

But O! to stand directly in the midst,
Below the scarred old rocks on either hand,
Low down in shadow, and from off the ground
To let the eye rise from the weedy grass
And slowly make acquaintance with the moss
And many-coloured lichens of the rock;
And with the hanging grass, which grows and
  sways,
Head downward, whispering softly to the breeze;
With vines that climb and vines that overfall
Luring the eye to follow the long curves,
Till high above I see the twisted roots,
And higher yet, like lines of silver light,
The overreaching stems that half across,

MY PLACE.

From either side the pathway, hold aslant
The longing separated birches there,
Whose quivering leaves attempt to blend in vain;
And higher yet, between them and beyond,
As if seen for the first time in my life,
Lo the blue sky! far off, but not too far!

Beyond the rocks are trees that overhang
Few wild flowers in the Spring, but in the Fall
Uncounted wealth of many-coloured leaves—
Old chestnut trees, and hickories and oaks,
Wound round with woodbine, overgrown with
    moss,
Under whose ample branches dogwoods grow.
In Winter I have seen them blotted out
By blurring snow-storms from the encroaching
    sky,
And on smooth lying snow have traced, how
    oft,
The still blue shadows of their thinnest twigs;

And in the Spring have seen them putting
forth,
And thrilled to see that first faint tender green
Above the rugged bark, as if I saw
Tears of mere tenderness upon the face
Of some stern fighter in a life-long war;
And in the Summer I have sat and mused
For hours beneath their dream-compelling leaves.

But in the Autumn love them most of all;
And that especially for four or five
Supreme old oaks and hickories, even now,
This third day of November, which retain
A glory that no others ever had.
The frequent maples, that last month fulfilled
The air with cheerfulness, are faded now
To brooding brown, or oftener yet become
Mere leaden outlines, stiff and cold; but here
Are hickories still with living golden leaves
Unblenching from the breezes, while around

The chestnut leaves are fluttering down in showers,
And even in places crackling under foot.

But the one tree which consecrates the place
With glorious beauty is a lonely oak
Which stands full in the sunlight, with a mass
Of quivering, clear, almost transparent leaves,
Which look like burning rubies in the air,
So red they are, so full of life and light.
No other autumn tree can match with this—
No scarlet maple among its golden mates,
No sumach, no, nor woodbine where it falls
O'er a gray rock in sunlight, shows a red
So clear, so pure, so ravishing as this—
Like light itself, a mystery, a charm:
One almost fears to see it pass away
With every movement of the hovering breeze;
But it remains, it lives and glows and grows,
And holds me like a sunset, till at last

I break away reluctantly, and turn
And turn again to see it yet once more,
Mingling its rubies with the glancing gold
Of sunlit leaves behind it, while the sky,
In sapphire flecks seen thro' the magic web,
Seems quivering with its motion like the sea.

But ere one passes from between the rocks,
He sees a gleam of brightness underneath,
Which tells him why the pathway all at once
Descends so swiftly, making haste to meet
The beckoning waters that it sees below.
And so its eagerness begets in me
An equal longing, and I hurry down,
And for a moment am amazed and blind
Before the rippling river as it flows
And flashes in the sunlight at my feet.

But, far off in the distance to the left,
Soon I begin to see a narrow shore

Which widens ever, till straight across I see
Broad sloping fields, and back of them the woods
That step by step rise up to mark the sky
With dark uneven fringes on the blue;
Then no more meadows for the waves to wash,
But a bare wall to beat against in vain
Of unassisted rock, which far away
Curves suddenly to meet, or seem to meet
The bending shore, and shut the river in,
So that all sails that pass me outward bound
Seem all at once to strangely disappear
As if the mountain took them, as of old
The Venusberg took Venus and her knight;
While those that come seem rising from the
    depths,
Like Flying-Dutchmen from another world.—
And yonder by the chestnut is My Place

It has two parts; the first, a grassy bank
Just on the border of a little wood

Of chestnut-trees, above a tiny pool
Of shallow water, from whose edge the grass
Slopes once again to meet the actual shore
(Its second part), than which I think there is
No better place to see and hear the waves,
And watch the noiseless changes of the clouds.

When I first found it 'twas a lovely day—
A lovely latter May-day, warm and bright—
A day for lying on the grass alone,
To watch and wonder at the tender leaves,
And breathe the fragrance of the kindred ground;
Over and back of me the breathing trees,
And over these, seen partly thro' the boughs,
The waveless sky, with little melting clouds;
Below, the shallow waters reproduced
The rocks and shrubs and overhanging trees,
And sky and clouds and butterflies and birds—
Its magic stillness broken only once
By magic music, where a thin lost rill,

MY PLACE.

From groping thro' the hiding grass, at last
Stole forth and found and fell into its lake,
With ripple and flash, like laughter heard and
    seen;
And then the river, seen without its shore,
Bright in the sunlight, rippled by the breeze;
Far off the incessant glances of a quick
Insufferable multitude of suns;
Nearer, a broad white band of blinding light,
Which made the waters just this side of it
Seem almost black with gloom, which when the
    sails
Touched they were changed, and in a moment
    gone,
Lost in the splendour of concealing light.

And many a morning since, upon the shore
Have I sat still and let the river flow
Unheeded, while I watched the silent clouds
On the transparent river of the air,

Like ruffled swans rejoicing in the breeze,
Whose motion was for music; or have tried
To name the unimaginable forms
Of all the cirri in the upper blue,
Pleased like a child to mark what flecks of foam,
What overfalling wool-white waves were there,
What misty beams, what thread-like lines of light,
What flying flashes of revolving fire,
What airy tongues of unpolluted flame,
What breathing Northern-lights, what Milky-ways,
What fairy frost-work, what gigantic ferns,
What cirri simply (I came back to that)—
Till into me insensibly the charm
Of all the loveliness of all the sky,
Its light, its joy, its clearness and its calm,
Stole like sweet music, ending in a cry
Of inexpressible desire, and passed.
And still the breeze just touched the lazy leaves,
And at my feet the seeming sleepy waves
Moved only as a dreamful sleeper breathes.

But there are days of quiet, when the calm
Seems not of dreaming, but of speechless thought,
And under all the quietness I feel,
I know what lurking restlessness is there,
That with the waking comes the war again.
And often as I sit and look across,
And contemplate the slow unyielding rocks,
Dead to the movement of the clouds and waves,
Their joy or pain, their hope or their despair,—
Oft as I sit alone and look at these,
The whole world changes, and at once my dreams
Born of the warm air and the whispering leaves,
Are scattered from me by the self-same thought
That crowds the waves to wear the rocks away;
Then what are dreams of things to be desired
To that desire of things to be denied,
Which pricks me to my feet and sets my face
With hungry pain against the little breeze?—
Longing to feel it change into a swift,
Indignant wind, which shall uprouse the waves

To fury, and the tree-tops to a grand
Dishevelled madness, while from woods to waves
The roar is answered, and my soul relieved
By lifting music from its want of wings,
And envy of the sea-gulls, where they fly
Wrestling the wind, insatiate of the storm.

Such winds I find here often in the Fall
Then not such clouds as but enhance the blue
Above the rippling river whitely sail
Nowhither smoothly, but rebellious shapes
Of writhing darkness, like the lower waves,
Rise raging and fall sullenly, blown on
And dashed against the inviolable sun;
Grandly they rise and grandly are thrust down,
The ragged foam-like edges wildly bright
With an unwelcome brightness, till at last—
As naturally as if the storm itself
Were but the inclusion of a central calm—

There comes a change; the uncertain wind
decides;
The trees still rock and roar and grind; the
waves
Still writhe and gnash and murmur unappeased;
The clouds still sway and struggle overhead;
But in the west a space of purer blue
(Heaven never is so purely blue as when
The heavy clouds are broken after rain)
Expects its glory from the setting sun,
And takes it, and the changing clouds no less
Take alien beauty, and I too am glad
After the storm, and with light step and heart
Can now walk homeward, having little need,
Lighted and shone upon by such a sky,
Of any God or Goddess, Friend or Love,
Except for thanks, except for sympathy.

AD AMICUM.

FORGIVE me if I seem to change and be
    Other than what you loved me for before;
What is not changed and changing? Ah! no
    more,
No more now in fresh morning meadows we
With songs may walk together, light and free,
But, thrust apart, too hardly measure o'er
A highway journey, in whose dust and roar
All things are altered that we hear and see:
What wonder then if I look dark and grim,
Soiled by the dust of this too dusty way?
What wonder if the eye grow strangely dim,
And the voice husky that was once so gay?
And yet I think the unforgotten hymn
Shall yet again be sung some not too distant
    day.

www.ingramcontent.com/pod-product-compliance
Lightning Source LLC
Chambersburg PA
CBHW020306170426

43202CB00008B/511